Turning Reviews into Revenue: A Step-By-Step Guide to Winning Customers Online

Peter Lockwood

Copyright © 2024 by Peter Lockwood
All rights reserved.
ISBN | 978-0-646-70586-6

Table of Contents

Turning Reviews Into Revenue: A Step-By-Step Guide To Winning Customers Online..v

The Value of Google Reviews 1
    Why Google Reviews Matter 2
    The Impact of Reviews on Local SEO..3
    The Power of Social Proof..4
    The Direct Link Between Reviews and Revenue 4
    Overview of What's to Come 5

Master the Basics 6
    Set Up Your Google Business Profile..8
    Optimise Your Google Business Profile for Reviews and Engagement 9
    Encourage Reviews with an Optimised Profile 10
    Avoid Common Mistakes When Setting Up Your Profile........11
    Conclusion: Set the Stage for Success 11

Build a Review Culture: How to Get Your First 100 Reviews 13
    Why Building a Review Culture Matters 14
    Conclusion: Getting Your First 100 Reviews.............................19

Incentivise and Encourage Reviews Legally and Ethically 21
    Understand Google's Guidelines..22
    How to Legally Encourage Reviews...23
    Use Non-Monetary Incentives to Encourage Reviews...........25
    Ethical Contests and Giveaways...26
    Reward Loyalty Without Violating Guidelines 26
    Conclusion: Ethical Encouragement Leads to Long-Term Success 27

Industry-Specific Strategies to Collect Reviews 28
    The Power of Asking: Why You Need to Request Reviews 29
    Restaurants and Hospitality Outlets 29
    Retail Stores...30
    Tradespeople and On-Site Services...31
    Health and Beauty Services 32
    Real Estate and Sales...33
    Professional Services (Lawyers, Accountants, Financial Advisors) 33
    Locations for Review Collection 34
    Conclusion: Asking is Key 35

Handle Negative Reviews Like a Pro **36**
    Why Negative Reviews Matter 37
    Conclusion: Negative Reviews are Opportunities in
    Disguise 42
Game Changing Automation Tools and Software **43**
    Why Automate Your Review Process? 44
    Types of Review Automation Tools 45
    How to Set Up Automated Review Requests 46
    Benefits of Automating Review Requests 48
    Best Practices for Using Automation Without Losing the
    Personal Touch 49
    Conclusion: Automate for Growth, But Keep It Personal 50
The Power of Visuals: Use Photos and Videos to
Drive Reviews **51**
    Why Visual Content Matters 52
    Conclusion: Visuals are a Gateway to More Reviews 57
Social Proof: Turn Google Reviews into Marketing Gold **58**
    What is Social Proof? 59
    Conclusion: Social Proof is Your Secret Weapon 65
Boost Local SEO with Google Reviews **66**
    What is Local SEO? 67
    How Google Reviews Influence Local SEO 67
    Conclusion: The Synergy Between Reviews and
    Local SEO 71
The Future of Google Reviews and Reputation Management **73**
    Trend 1: Video and Voice Reviews Gaining Popularity 74
    Trend 2: The Integration of Augmented Reality (AR) in Review
    Experiences 75
    Trend 3: Reputation Management as a Core Business
    Function 76
    Trend 4: The Role of Blockchain in Authenticating
    Reviews 77
    Conclusion: Embrace the Future of Reviews and Reputation
    Management 78
Bring It All Together With Review Builder Pro **80**
    Automating the Review Process 81
    Managing Negative Reviews with Ease 81
    Bringing Social Proof to Your Website and Social Media 82

Comprehensive Analytics for Data-Driven Decisions 82
  Simplifying SEO and Review Management 82
  The Time-Saving Benefits of Review Builder Pro 83
Conclusion.. **84**
Author's Note: New Software Arriving Early 2025 – Review Builder GO **87**
Please Leave a Review **88**
Author Bio **89**

Turning Reviews Into Revenue: A Step-By-Step Guide To Winning Customers Online

Introduction

Online reviews are a powerful tool for businesses to attract new customers, build trust and maintain their reputation. Whether you're a small local shop, a large enterprise, or a service provider, the opinions and feedback of your customers can make or break your business. After all, potential customers only need a simple search to see what others are saying about your business—and their buying decisions are often influenced by those reviews.

According to a recent study published in *The World Financial Review,* titled "How Reviews Impact Your Sales", 82% of people base their choice of a new local business on Google reviews, which shows how important online feedback is for the success of a business in every industry. However, reviews are not only gathered to build your credibility. The objective should be to create a lasting, positive online presence that shows potential customers the value of what you have to offer.

Whether you're trying to figure out how to establish an online presence or looking to optimise your review strategy, the chapters in this book will give you practical insights to help you navigate the world of online reviews. My aim is to guide you step by step through the strategies necessary to build your reputation, increase positive feedback and ultimately, turn reviews into revenue.

You'll learn how to:

- set up and optimise your Google Business Profile to encourage reviews
- develop a review collection strategy to generate consistent, authentic feedback
- handle negative reviews professionally and turn them into opportunities for improvement

- leverage the power of automation tools to streamline the review process
- use reviews to boost your local SEO ranking and social media marketing.

In addition to these strategies, I will introduce you to Review Builder Pro, a tool designed to automate the process of requesting, collecting and managing reviews. You'll learn how to save valuable time, protect the reputation of your business and attract new customers by using this platform. In the spirit of full disclosure, I confess that I am the owner of Review Builder Pro and throughout this book I'll share how you can grow your business by using the power of reviews, while also automating the process.

Before we start on the journey to grow your business with customer reviews, a gentle reminder that if you don't ask for reviews, you will reduce your chances of getting them quite considerably. But with the right strategy in place, you'll create a steady flow of feedback that builds trust, boosts your SEO rankings and drives more business to your door.

The Value of Google Reviews

The Value of Google Reviews

The success of a business no longer depends solely on traditional marketing tactics or word-of-mouth recommendations. However, a new form of word-of-mouth now dominates: online reviews. Of these, Google reviews stand out as one of the most powerful tools to attract new customers and build trust. If you're a business owner, mastering the art of generating and managing Google reviews can be a game changer.

Why Google Reviews Matter

Imagine you're looking for a restaurant, a hair salon, or a contractor for home improvements. You get out your phone, open Google and search for options in your area. What's the first thing you see? That's right—a map and a list of businesses, each with a star rating, the number of reviews for that business, and a snapshot of some recent feedback. This is the first impression most potential customers will have of your business. The researchers of a study published in the international *Journal of Retailing and Consumer Services* found that 84% of consumers place as much trust in online reviews as they do in personal recommendations.

Simply put, Google reviews are influential because they:

- **Build trust and credibility**
  Customers tend to trust a business with positive reviews from real people.

- **Improve local SEO**
  The more reviews you have—and the higher your star rating—the more likely you are to rank higher in local searches, especially in Google's coveted "Local Pack".

- **Influence purchasing decisions**
  Positive reviews are the social proof that reassures customers they're making the right choice.

But why Google reviews specifically? Google is by far the most used search engine globally, capturing over 90% of all search queries. Reviews on other platforms like Trustpilot or Facebook are important too, but Google reviews directly influence how often your business appears in people's search results and maps. Additionally, you get unparalleled visibility because the reviews are integrated with Google Maps and Search.

The Impact of Reviews on Local SEO

Local SEO maximises your online presence, thereby attracting more business from local searches. One of the key factors that influence local SEO is the quantity, quality and consistency of your Google reviews.

Here's how Google reviews affect your local SEO:

- **Review Quantity**
  The more reviews your business has, the better. Google recognises that a business with a large number of reviews has social proof, which in turn indicates its credibility.

- **Review Quality**
  A five-**star** rating is a clear signal of customer satisfaction, but stars are not all that matter. Google's algorithm also looks at the content of the reviews. Reviews with keywords relevant to your business and location can further boost your search rankings.

- **Review Velocity**
  How often you get new reviews matters. A steady stream of fresh feedback signals to Google that your business is active and engages with customers.

When your business has a high number of positive Google reviews, it not only appears higher in search results, but could also feature in the Google Local Pack—which is that top section on the search page showing a map and three of the most relevant local businesses. Getting into this pack is a powerful way to increase your visibility and drive traffic to your business.

The Power of Social Proof

Customers want to feel confident that they're making the right choice when selecting a product or service. When they are not sure of themselves, they look at what other people do before they make a decision. Bestselling author and business psychologist Robert Cialdini introduced the term 'social proof' to describe this behaviour of people to be persuaded by the actions of others. In the context of business, this means that potential customers look to existing reviews as proof of what their experience is likely to be.

Google reviews provide that much-needed validation because of:

- **Star Ratings**
  A high average rating translates to high levels of trust. In fact, businesses with 4 stars and above are more likely to attract new customers than those with lower ratings.

- **Review Volume**
  A single five-star review is great, but a business with 100 reviews—many of which are positive—comes across as more reliable than one with only one or two reviews—however high they may be.

- **Detailed Reviews**
  Customers appreciate reading honest, detailed feedback. Reviews that highlight specific aspects of the customer experience—such as product quality, customer service, or delivery times—provide a more convincing picture of the nature of your business.

The way to harness the power of social proof is discussed in detail in a later chapter, but until then bear in mind that social proof is often the tipping point in a customer's decision-making process. A business with a strong Google review profile will experience a notable increase in both foot traffic and online transactions.

The Direct Link Between Reviews and Revenue

The reason businesses are so focused on gathering reviews is that they have a direct impact on revenue. Professor Michael Luca of the Harvard Business School determined that just a one-star increase on your review rating can lead to a 5–9% increase in revenue. The reason is that higher-rated businesses not only attract more customers, but they can also charge more. Customers are willing to pay a premium when they feel confident in the quality and reputation of a business.

On the other hand, negative reviews handled poorly can have a devastating impact on your business. A succession of bad reviews can scare away potential customers, hurt your local SEO ranking and damage your reputation. That is the reason your focus should not only be on getting more reviews but you should also manage and respond to reviews effectively—something I'll cover in detail later in this book.

Overview of What's to Come

Now that we've established why Google reviews are critical to the growth of your business, the rest of this book introduces practical strategies to help you gather, manage and leverage reviews to their full potential. Whether you're just starting out or looking to improve your existing business approach, you'll find tips and insights that can help you build a review pipeline, attract more customers and boost your revenue.

The next chapter looks at how to set up and optimise your Google Business Profile to ensure that you're fully prepared to start collecting reviews and improving your online presence.

Master the Basics

Master the Basics

Before you can start collecting those glowing reviews, you should lay a solid foundation. That foundation is your Google Business Profile (GBP). Without an optimised profile, even the most positive customer experiences may not translate into the reviews and visibility your business needs. In this chapter, I'll walk you through the steps you should take to optimise your profile so that your business is easy to find and encourages customers to leave reviews.

What is a Google Business Profile?

A Google Business Profile is the identity of your business on Google. People see this when they search for your company, whether on Google Search or Google Maps. It displays key information like your business name, location, operating hours, contact details, website and, importantly, your customers' reviews. A well-optimised profile gives potential customers all the information they need to make an informed decision quickly and easily.

An optimised GBP is necessary because it:

- **Increases visibility.** Google favours well-optimised business profiles in search results and maps.

- **Attracts more reviews.** A clear and professional profile encourages customers to engage, which includes leaving reviews.

- **Provides useful information.** Customers can quickly find your business, contact you, or visit your physical location.

Set Up Your Google Business Profile

If you haven't claimed your Google Business Profile yet, here are the first steps to get you started:

1. **Create or Claim Your Profile**

    1. Go to Google Business Profile and click "Manage Now".
    2. If your business already exists in Google's database, you'll be prompted to claim it. If not, you can create a new profile by filling in your business information.
    3. Use your official business name and ensure all details are accurate, including your category (e.g., "restaurant," "plumber," or "hair salon").

2. **Add Your Business Information**

    1. **Business Name**: Use the exact name of your business as registered.
    2. **Business Category**: Choose the most appropriate category for your business. This determines the type of searches you'll appear in. You can add secondary categories later if applicable.
    3. **Location**: If you have a physical storefront, ensure your address is accurate. If you don't have a public-facing address (e.g., if you're a home-based business or offer services at customer locations), you can choose to hide your address and simply list your service areas.
    4. **Contact Details**: Include a phone number and a website URL if applicable. Ensure this information is correct, as Google often uses these details to verify your business.

3. **Verify Your Business**

    Once your profile is complete, you must verify your business. Google formerly sent a postcard to your business address with a verification code, but other methods, like phone or email or video verification, may also be required depending on your business type.

Verifying your profile is a necessary step—without verification, your profile won't appear in searches, and you won't be able to manage reviews or edit business details.

Optimise Your Google Business Profile for Reviews and Engagement

Now that your profile is live, it's time to optimise it so that it attracts more attention and more reviews. Here's how to make sure your profile stands out from the crowd:

1. **Complete Every Section of Your Profile**

    The probability that potential customers will see a fully filled-out profile is higher than when a profile only has basic information. This includes information like your business hours, service areas, business description and holiday hours. Use the "Business Description" section to tell customers who you are, what you offer and why they should choose you. This should be a concise but informative summary of your business, ideally focusing on your unique selling points (USPs).

2. **Add High-Quality Photos**

    Photos are one of the most engaging elements of a Google Business Profile. According to Google themselves, businesses with photos get 35% more clicks to their website and 42% more requests for directions compared to those without. Add professional-looking photos of your storefront, products, services and even behind-the-scenes shots to humanise your business. Encourage your customers to add photos when they leave reviews. Customer-generated images have authenticity and generate trust.

3. **Select Relevant Business Attributes**

    Google lets you select "attributes" that describe your business. These are important for searches, as they can help potential customers find you based on their specific needs. For example, if your business is "wheelchair accessible" or offers Wi-Fi, be sure to include these in your profile.

4. **Add a Q&A Section**

    The questions and answers section is a great opportunity to engage with potential customers directly. Anyone can ask a question about your business, and you (or other users) can provide answers. Be proactive and answer frequently asked questions upfront. This not only helps you control the narrative but also shows customers that you are responsive and informative.

Encourage Reviews with an Optimised Profile

An optimised profile does more than just make your business look professional—it also makes it easier for customers to leave reviews. Here's how to use your profile to encourage feedback:

1. **Make it Easy to Leave a Review**

    Google encourages you to create a custom review link that you can share with customers. By providing a direct link to your review page, you remove any obstacle customers might encounter in finding where to leave their feedback. Add this link to your email signatures, text messages, social media and even receipts.

2. **Respond to Reviews—Both Positive and Negative**

    Responding to reviews shows potential customers that you value feedback and are willing to engage with them. Be sure to reply to positive reviews with a personalised message that acknowledges their satisfaction. A simple "Thank you for your feedback!" can go a long way in reinforcing goodwill.

Negative reviews, on the other hand, require tact. Respond professionally, offer solutions and ask the customer to reach out privately to resolve the issue. This not only shows potential customers that you care but also gives you a chance to turn a negative experience into a positive one. AI can assist with this, as well as enable you to take the emotion out of your replies to negative reviews. I'll cover more on this later.

3. **Encourage Check-Ins and Engagement**

    Customers who engage with your profile by checking in or uploading photos are more inclined to leave reviews. If you have a physical location, offer a small incentive for customers who check in via Google. You can advertise this in-store with a small sign or mention it on your receipts.

Avoid Common Mistakes When Setting Up Your Profile

Even though setting up a Google Business Profile is relatively straightforward, there are a few common mistakes to avoid:

- **Inconsistent Information**
  Make sure your business details (name, address, phone number) are consistent across all online platforms, not just Google. Inconsistencies can hurt your local SEO ranking.

- **Ignoring Reviews**
  A neglected profile with unanswered reviews, especially to negative ones, can turn potential customers away.

- **Not Updating Regularly**
  Keep your profile current. If your hours change, you move locations, or you offer new services, update your Google Business Profile immediately.

Conclusion: Set the Stage for Success

Setting up and optimising your Google Business Profile is the first step in your journey to increased reviews for business growth. A well-optimised profile not only improves your visibility in local search results but also encourages customer engagement and reviews, giving you the necessary foundation to collect valuable feedback.

If you need help to set up and/or optimise your Google Business Profile, I can provide this service for you. Please scan the QR code on the back of this book to make an appointment.

In the next chapter, we'll go through how to build a review culture within your business, ensuring that gathering reviews becomes a consistent and manageable part of your business operations.

Build a Review Culture: How to Get Your First 100 Reviews

Build a Review Culture: How to Get Your First 100 Reviews

Now that your Google Business Profile is fully optimised, it's time to focus on one of the most critical aspects of turning reviews into profit: getting them in the first place. A well-optimised profile with no reviews doesn't carry much weight in the eyes of potential customers. Reviews are the social proof that signals to customers that your business is trustworthy and worth their attention.

In this chapter, we'll look at how to build a review culture within your business, so that the process of leaving, collecting and responding to feedback becomes second nature for you, your team and your customers.

Why Building a Review Culture Matters

Businesses that regularly collect reviews actively prioritise customer feedback as part of their operations. This doesn't happen by accident—it requires intention and strategy. A review culture means that your team knows the value of reviews, your customers feel encouraged to leave feedback and your business benefits from the continuous flow of customer opinions.

Fostering a review culture is important because it:

- **Boosts Customer Trust**

    Customers trust businesses with a lot of fresh and relevant reviews. This creates a cycle where positive reviews lead to more customers and more customers lead to more reviews.

- **Sustains SEO Benefits**

    Google rewards businesses that receive consistent reviews by pushing them higher in search rankings. The more reviews you get over time, the more your business will stay visible.

- **Fosters Internal Improvement**

    Reviews, whether positive or negative, give you valuable insights into how your business is performing from the customer's perspective. This information can be used to improve weak areas and maintain your strengths.

- **Builds Team Confidence**

    Having a structured process for obtaining reviews and training your team in doing so will build team confidence in asking customers to leave reviews. It becomes part of the everyday business process in the same way that customers are asked to pay at the register.

Step 1: Create a System for Requesting Reviews

A systematic approach is the key to getting more reviews. Hoping that customers will leave feedback without any prompting from your side usually leads to disappointment. Instead, build a process that seamlessly integrates review requests into your business operations. Here are some steps to create a simple, effective system:

1. **Train Your Team to Ask for Reviews**

    - Train your staff to politely ask customers for reviews, either at the point of sale or immediately after providing a service. Make sure they understand the importance of reviews to your business.

    - Teach them to be direct but not pushy. For example, a request like *"We'd love to hear about your experience. Would you mind leaving us a review on Google?"* is both polite and effective.

    - Encourage your team to target customers who seem especially happy, as they will be favourably inclined to leave positive feedback.

- Physical devices such as Tap and Review cards, coasters and counter signs make this process very easy.

Remember, if you don't ask, you don't get.

2. **Use Email and SMS Follow-Ups**

    - After every sale or service, send a follow-up email or SMS thanking the customer and including a direct link to where they can leave a review on Google. Timing is critical—send the message within 24 to 48 hours while the experience is still fresh in their minds.

    - Keep the message short and friendly. Here's an example: *Thank you for choosing [Business Name]! We hope you enjoyed your experience. If you have a moment, we'd love it if you shared your thoughts on Google. Your feedback helps us improve and reach more customers. [Insert review link here].*

    - Make sure the review process is as easy as possible. Include clear instructions, and always provide a direct link to your Google review page.

Note: Review Builder Pro can automate this process for you. Please scan the QR code on the back of this book for a free trial.

3. **Provide Physical Reminders**

    - If you operate a physical business, include reminders to leave reviews on your printed receipts, packaging, or flyers. You could add a simple call to action like, *"Loved our service? Tell us on Google!"*

    - For service-based businesses, consider leaving a thank-you card with a QR code that links directly to your review page after completing a job. This personal touch not only provides a better customer experience but also encourages them to share feedback.

Step 2: Incentivise Reviews Without Violating Google's Policies

Although offering incentives can be an effective way to gather more reviews, make sure that you do so ethically and within Google's guidelines. Google explicitly prohibits businesses from offering rewards or discounts in exchange for reviews, as this can lead to biased or dishonest feedback. However, there are still creative ways to encourage customers to leave reviews without crossing the line.

We will cover this topic in greater detail in the next chapter, however some incentives include:

- hosting a monthly review contest

- using non-monetary incentives

- encouraging feedback through loyalty programs

Step 3: Automate Review Requests

If asking for reviews feels overwhelming, you're in luck—automation can make this process much easier and more efficient. Several tools and software platforms can help you streamline your review collection efforts:

1. **Use a CRM with Automated Review Requests**

    - Many customer relationship management (CRM) platforms have the option to set up automated emails or text messages after each transaction that prompt customers to leave reviews. This ensures that every customer receives a timely request without you having to manually reach out.

    - Set rules within your CRM to send follow-ups at an optimal time for your industry. For example, if you're a restaurateur, you might want to send a review request the day after they visited your eatery. If you're a contractor, it might make sense to follow up a week after the job is completed.

2. Leverage Review Management Tools

Several specialised tools—like Review Builder Pro—not only automate review requests but also facilitates management and responding to reviews from one platform. Review Builder Pro integrates seamlessly with most CRMs to provide a streamlined review management package. It can also filter out potential bad reviews, thereby protecting the reputation of your business.

These tools can track which customers received a review request and follow up with those who haven't responded yet. They also monitor new reviews in real time so you can quickly address any negative feedback and can use AI to make the process quicker and less emotional.

Step 4: Encourage Customer Engagement Through Social Media

Your social media channels are powerful tools for promoting reviews. By engaging with customers on platforms like Facebook, Instagram and X (formerly Twitter), you can create a seamless connection between social engagement and Google reviews.

1. Share Positive Reviews

- Whenever you receive a glowing review, share it on your social media accounts with a thank-you message. This not only shows appreciation to the reviewer but also encourages others to follow suit. Customers who see that you value feedback are more likely to leave a review.

- For example, you could post a screenshot of a review and add a caption like: *"Thank you, [customer name], for the fantastic review! We're so happy you enjoyed [product/service]! Have you had a great experience with us? Share your thoughts on Google here: [Insert link]."*

Use Review Builder Pro from your desktop or mobile to share your reviews across all social platforms with the click of a button.

2. **Host Engagement Campaigns**

    - Run social media campaigns asking your followers to share their experiences on Google. Create posts that encourage customers to share their thoughts and remind them of how valuable their feedback is for your business.

    - Use hashtags like #CustomerLove or #ThankYouThursday to build engagement and make it fun for customers to participate.

Step 5: Keep the Momentum Going

Once you start collecting reviews, the goal is to keep the momentum going. Building a review culture is not a one-time effort, but a continuous practice. Here's how to ensure that reviews remain a key part of your business operations:

1. **Make Review Collection a Part of Your Business Process**

    Whether you're onboarding new customers, finishing up a service, or selling a product, make sure that requesting reviews is a standard step in your process. Include it in your sales scripts, after-sales emails and team training. Every interaction with a customer is an opportunity to ask for a review.

2. **Measure Your Success**

    Track how many reviews you collect each week or month. Use tools like Google Business Profile Insights or review management platforms like Review Builder Pro to monitor the frequency and quality of the feedback you receive. Set goals for review collection—whether it's reaching your first 100 reviews or increasing your review count by 10% each quarter.

Conclusion: Getting Your First 100 Reviews

Getting your first 100 reviews may seem like a daunting task, but by following these steps and building a review culture within your business, you'll start seeing results in no time. Whether you ask directly, automate the process, or engage customers through social media, creating a system for reviews ensures that your business constantly gathers fresh feedback.

In the next chapter, I'll show you how to incentivise and encourage customers to leave reviews in ethical and creative ways—while staying within Google's guidelines.

Incentivise and Encourage Reviews Legally and Ethically

Incentivise and Encourage Reviews Legally and Ethically

Now that you've begun building a review culture and implemented a system to collect feedback, it's time to consider how customers can be motivated and incentivised to leave reviews. However, when you encourage reviews, it's extremely important to tread carefully. Google has strict policies about offering direct incentives in exchange for positive reviews. Violating these rules can result in your reviews being removed or, worse, your business profile being penalised.

In this chapter, I'll show you some examples on how to ethically and legally encourage reviews without compromising your integrity or risking the online reputation of your business.

Understand Google's Guidelines

Before we look at ways to encourage reviews, we should first understand Google's policies. Google explicitly prohibits offering incentives such as discounts, gifts, or rewards in exchange for positive reviews. Their guidelines clearly state:

- **No financial incentives**

    You may not offer money, discounts, or freebies in exchange for a review. This applies whether you're asking for a positive or negative review.

- **No misleading or fake reviews**

    You should not post reviews of your own business or ask anyone to do so when you provided them with no service or product.

- **No conditional offers**

    You may not offer something of value only if the review is positive.

Any attempt to manipulate reviews, such as directly paying for them or incentivising them improperly, can have serious consequences.

Your entire Google Business Profile could be suspended, or your reviews could be flagged and removed. That's why ethical and creative approaches are a must.

How to Legally Encourage Reviews

The key to ethically encouraging reviews is to make it easy and attractive for customers to share their experiences without directly incentivising them for the act itself. Instead of offering rewards, focus on creating a memorable experience and giving customers a nudge to leave feedback. Here's how you can do this:

1. **Create a Memorable Experience That Deserves a Review**

    The first and most effective strategy to get reviews is to deliver exceptional customer service. If you consistently provide a positive experience, customers will naturally want to share their thoughts with others. Your customers should be so delighted that they feel compelled to leave feedback.

    Consider personal touches—a hand-written thank-you note, surprise gifts for loyal customers, or going above and beyond the norm to meet their needs. When customers feel that they received something extra or unexpected, they'll want to leave a review in most cases.

2. **Ask at the Right Time**

    Timing is everything when asking for review requests. You want to ask for a review when the experience is fresh in the customer's mind and their emotions are positive.

    As I have said before, the optimal timing is often different for each industry. For example:

    - If you own a restaurant, ask for reviews right after customers finished their meal. You could hand out a card with a QR code linked to your Google review page with their receipt. We will discuss this further in a later chapter.

- If you're a service-based business, send a follow-up email the day after you completed the service to ensure that the customer has had time to reflect on their experience. Review Builder Pro can automate this process for you.

Use your business's natural touchpoints to integrate review requests in a non-intrusive way.

3. **Leverage Your Brand's Storytelling**

   People love to be part of a story. One effective and ethical way to encourage reviews is to let customers know how much their feedback helps your business grow. You can communicate this by sharing personal anecdotes about how reviews have helped you improve your services or reach new customers. For example: *"Your review helps small businesses like ours continue to grow and serve more customers like you. We truly appreciate your feedback!"* Make their act of leaving a review an integral element of your larger mission, so that customers feel they are contributing to your success story.

4. **Make the Review Process Simple**

   Customers are less likely to leave reviews if the process is complicated. Provide them with a direct link to your Google review page and give them clear instructions. QR codes are particularly effective if you have a physical location. These can be printed on receipts, business cards, or table tents in a restaurant setting. Near Field Communication (NFC) Tap and Review cards are particularly effective in physical locations because your customer only has to tap their mobile phone on the card for your Google review page to open directly.

   Additionally, include helpful prompts to make it easier for customers to leave meaningful feedback. For instance, suggest what they might write about by asking:

   - "What did you enjoy most about our service?"
   - "How did our product help you solve a problem?"

Giving customers specific things to comment on makes the task less daunting and increases the likelihood that they leave thoughtful reviews.

Use Non-Monetary Incentives to Encourage Reviews

Even though direct financial incentives are prohibited, there are other ways to motivate customers to leave feedback that comply with Google's policies. Here are some effective non-monetary methods that will generate engagement:

1. **Create a Review Wall**

    Giving prominence to your reviewers on a public platform, such as a "Review Wall" on your website or social media account, can act as a motivator. Let your customers know that their review might be featured on your website or in a monthly social media shoutout. For example, you could have a section on your site titled "Our Happy Customers" and display their reviews along with their names (with permission). Public recognition gives people a sense of importance and ownership in your brand's story.

    This feature can be set up and automated through Review Builder Pro.

2. **Engage Customers in a Social Cause**

    Tie your review campaign to a social cause that your customers care about. For example, let them know that for every review they leave, your business will make a small donation to a local charity or plant a tree. This aligns your review collection with a purpose and makes customers feel good about leaving feedback. Be transparent about the impact: *"Help us support [Charity Name]! For every review we receive this month, we'll donate [amount] to [cause]."*

3. **Build Customer Loyalty Through Engagement**

    Engage with your most loyal customers by offering them early access to new products or services in exchange for honest feedback. This type of exclusive access rewards them without monetising the review. Create a loyalty program that offers rewards for frequent purchases or referrals, and gently remind members of how valuable their feedback is. This soft approach encourages customers to leave reviews without feeling as if they're being coerced into complying with your request.

Ethical Contests and Giveaways

Running a contest can be a creative way to encourage customers to engage with your brand and leave reviews. However, make sure the contest complies with Google's rules.

1. **Host a Monthly Giveaway**

   Consider holding a monthly contest where everyone who leaves a review is entered into a draw to win a prize. Be careful to emphasise that the quality of the review does not affect their eligibility—they're entered whether their review is positive or negative. This approach encourages honest feedback while still offering an incentive for participation. To stay transparent, include the terms and conditions of the contest in your messaging.

2. **Social Media Shoutouts**

   Run a fun campaign where customers who leave reviews get a chance to be featured on your social media channels. Whether it's a simple shoutout or a dedicated post celebrating their review, public recognition can be a powerful motivator. This type of campaign creates a win-win situation—customers get their moment of fame, and you get authentic reviews. Don't forget that you should always get the customer's permission first!

Reward Loyalty Without Violating Guidelines

Even though you can't pay customers directly for leaving reviews, you can reward them for their loyalty in ways that indirectly encourage feedback. By focusing on long-term relationships, you create a cycle of loyalty that leads to reviews:

1. **Surprise and Delight Your Customers**

   Sometimes, surprising a loyal customer with a small token of appreciation—without asking for a review—can naturally lead to positive feedback. When customers feel valued, they will happily talk about their experience. This could be anything from offering a complimentary service to sending a thank-you note.

2. **Offer Feedback Loops**

   Provide opportunities for customers to give feedback in multiple ways. If a customer isn't comfortable leaving a public review, ask for feedback through a private survey, then follow up by asking if they would be willing to share that feedback on Google. This two-step approach can help ease customers into the review process, especially if they're hesitant about sharing their thoughts publicly at first.

Conclusion: Ethical Encouragement Leads to Long-Term Success

Encouraging reviews ethically requires that you balance creativity with respect for both your customers and Google's guidelines. You can grow your reviews without risking your online reputation by focusing on creating positive experiences, simplifying the review process and using the above non-monetary incentives.

In the next chapter I'll cover off with some tips and tricks on how specific industries can improve their opportunities to increase reviews.

Industry-Specific Strategies to Collect Reviews

Industry-Specific Strategies to Collect Reviews

I already gave two examples in previous chapters to illustrate that the approach you take when collecting customer reviews should be tailored to your industry. Every business interacts with its customers differently, therefore the most effective way to gather reviews will vary depending on your sector. This chapter will give an overview of industry-specific methods for collecting reviews and an explanation how to leverage tools like QR codes and NFC (Near Field Communication) technology to make the process simple and efficient.

The Power of Asking: Why You Need to Request Reviews

Before we begin to go through specific methods, I really want to emphasise one key point: you will have to ask for reviews in one form or another. As with many things in business, if you don't ask, you may not get. Customers may love your service or product, but unless they are prompted, they may not think to leave a review. Asking for reviews—whether in person or through automated prompts—is one of the most important factors with which you increase the quantity of feedback your business receives. Simply put, the more you ask, the more reviews you will get.

Restaurants and Hospitality Outlets

In the restaurant and hospitality industry, reviews play a massive role in attracting new customers. People trust peer recommendations, especially regarding food and service experiences. The key to getting reviews is a process that is as convenient as possible for your patrons.

Effective Methods:

- **NFC Tap and Review cards and/or coasters** that are placed on each table. Customers can tap their smartphones on the card or coaster to be directed to your review page without even scanning a QR code.

- Include **QR codes on menus** that link directly to your business profile where customers can leave their review. This is a great way to catch customers while they are still seated and reflecting on their dining experience.

- Use **posters and table tents,** or other tabletop displays, with QR codes and a prompt asking for reviews. Position them in areas where customers can easily spot them, such as the front desk, waiting areas, or by the exit.

- Add a **QR code on printed receipts**, so customers can leave a review after they left the restaurant.

- Put a **small card in the bill wallet** with NFC or QR code when giving the bill to the customer. The front of house staff should let patrons know it's there and ask them to kindly leave a review.

- Have **staff carry a NFC Tap and Review card** and ask the customer to review their experience just before they clear the table. The card can be attached to a retractable ID card holder.

NFC Tap and Review cards reduce the number of actions required by your customer, making it much easier for them to leave a review than when using a QR code. The user only needs to tap their phone, even if locked, to be referred to the review page prompt. With a QR code, the user must unlock their phone, open the camera app, point the camera at the code and click on a prompt to open the review page before they can leave a review.

The key is to make it as easy as possible for customers to leave reviews and to choose the right time to ask. This will considerably reduce rejections and within a minute or so your customer can go about whatever they were doing, such as socialising or leaving the venue.

Retail Stores

In retail, timing and convenience are equally important when asking for reviews. By placing prompts in high-traffic areas of your store, you increase the likelihood that customers will leave feedback.

Effective Methods:

- Place a **NFC Tap and Review counter stand at the checkout**, preferably placed in a location that customers can't miss.

- Small **display stands** at the cash register, with a QR code and a polite message asking for a review, can catch customers' attention while they're finalising their purchase.

- Include QR codes on **printed receipts**, **leaflet inserts** and even on **shopping bags**, encouraging customers to leave a review after their shopping experience. This gives them the option to scan and leave feedback at their convenience post-purchase.

- Hand out **business or loyalty cards** with a QR code for leaving reviews. Customers are likely to keep these cards in their wallets, increasing the chances of getting reviews later on.

Reviews for retail outlets will be more about the customer's experience of your store and the customer service you provide, rather than the product itself.

Tradespeople and On-Site Services

For businesses that offer services in clients' homes or at various sites (such as plumbers, electricians, painters, landscapers, or HVAC technicians), the best time to ask for a review is soon after the job is complete, when the customer is still satisfied with the service.

Effective Methods:

- Tradespeople should carry **NFC Tap and Review cards** with them, making it easy for customers to tap the card and leave a review on the spot. This is especially helpful for technicians or contractors who have just completed a service.

- Display the **QR code on your mobile phone**. If customers don't have time for a conversation, simply ask them to scan the code on your phone and leave a quick review.

- Include a **QR code on your business cards**. After you've completed a job, hand the customer your card and let them know they can scan it to leave feedback.

- Tradespeople should politely ask the customer **in person** to leave a review before they leave the site. Many customers will appreciate the reminder and will gladly follow through.

- Attach **stickers with QR codes** on service paperwork, job completion forms, or even tools/equipment left on-site for larger projects.

- Alternatively, sending **SMS and/or email requests for reviews with a review link or QR Code** is effective if it's not possible to ask for them in person.

Health and Beauty Services

For professionals working in health and beauty, such as salons, spas, dentists, doctors, tattoo artists, or gym coaches, reviews are vital for building trust and attracting new clients. A personal ask and a convenient review process will boost the chances of receiving reviews.

Effective Methods:

- Place posters with a QR code or NFC Tap and Review stand in the **reception area or at each workstation**, prompting clients to leave a review. Returning customers can scan or tap while waiting for their appointment.

- Include **QR codes on printed receipts, invoices, or appointment reminder cards**. This ensures that clients are reminded to leave feedback, even after their session is over.

- Distribute **flyers with QR codes** that clients can take with them after their visit. This is particularly effective for services that rely on repeat customers, such as personal trainers or hairstylists.

- Beauty professionals and healthcare providers can **personally ask clients** to leave reviews, especially at the end of a session or appointment when the client is feeling satisfied with the results. The professional can carry a NFC Tap and Review card with them to make it easier for the customer to leave a review.

Real Estate and Sales

In industries where trust and credibility are paramount—such as real estate, car dealerships and luxury goods—reviews can be a powerful tool for building reputation and closing sales.

Effective Methods:

- Real estate agents and car salespeople should include **QR codes on their business cards**. After a successful sale or property viewing, ask the client to leave a review by scanning the code.

- After a major purchase or sale, send a **follow-up SMS or email that includes a link or QR code** for customers to leave a review. Personalised emails go a long way in encouraging customers to leave thoughtful feedback.

- Include a **review request flyer** in post-sale or follow-up documentation. This can be particularly effective for businesses that rely on long-term customer relationships, such as estate agents or insurance brokers.

Professional Services (Lawyers, Accountants, Financial Advisors)

In professional service industries, where long-term relationships are often formed, asking for reviews may feel out of place. However, there are still plenty of discreet ways to gather feedback without coming across as pushy.

Effective Methods:

- If your business sends direct mail—such as tax-time reminders or post-case follow-ups—include a **flyer with a QR code** asking for a review.

- After a major consultation or sale, send a **follow-up email that includes a link or QR code** for customers to leave a review.

- For professionals like accountants or lawyers who regularly send invoices, include **a QR code on printed or digital invoices** so clients can leave feedback easily.

- Place a **poster** with a review request and QR code and/or an NFC Tap and Review coaster, cards or counter stand **in your office reception or waiting room**. This subtle prompt encourages clients to leave feedback while they wait for appointments or consultations.

Locations for Review Collection

Here is a summary of effective locations where you can place review prompts (such as QR codes, NFC Tap and Review cards, coasters, counter stands or posters) to maximise review collection across various industries:

- In-store/office posters
- Table tents, tabletops (for restaurants or cafes)
- Front door or window
- Point of sale, checkout counter
- Stickers (especially for deliveries)
- Flyers and inserts
- Receipts or invoices
- Shopping bags
- Delivery bags (especially food delivery bags)
- Business and loyalty cards
- Reception areas
- Service areas
- Business cards
- Websites

No matter where you put the review collection prompt, it should always be at a "post-service" location, in other words for customers who already experienced your goods or services. For example, it is less effective having a QR code or Tap and Review card or counter stand at a café where a customer pays when they order instead of paying after their meal. Customers will be highly unlikely to leave a review if they don't know whether your product or service is any good.

Conclusion: Asking is Key

Regardless of the industry, the key to successfully collecting reviews is to ask for them. No matter how effective your strategy is or how easy you make the process, the probability that a customer leaves a review is much higher if they've been asked directly. Whether you use in-person requests, QR codes, NFC Tap and Review cards, coasters, counter stands or SMS/email follow-ups, don't be afraid to ask for reviews. After all, if you don't ask, you don't get.

In the next chapter, we'll focus on how to handle negative reviews like a pro—turning what could be a setback into an opportunity for growth and improved customer relationships.

Handle Negative Reviews Like a Pro

Handle Negative Reviews Like a Pro

No business, no matter how excellent their services or products, can escape negative reviews entirely. At some point, a customer will be dissatisfied, and they may choose to express their frustration online. While it might feel disheartening to see a less-than-glowing review, keep in mind that negative reviews can actually be opportunities for growth. How you respond to them can make a significant difference in how your business is perceived.

In this chapter, we'll discuss how to handle negative reviews professionally and turn them into valuable insights that not only protect your reputation but can also strengthen your customer relationships.

Why Negative Reviews Matter

While positive reviews are ideal, negative reviews are inevitable. Here's why they matter more than you might think:

- **Builds Credibility**

    A business with only perfect reviews could appear too good to be true. A few negative reviews amidst mostly positive feedback creates a more realistic image of your business and gives your credibility a boost.

- **Shows Transparency**

    How you respond to criticism is just as important as the review itself. Potential customers often look at how a business handles complaints to gauge its professionalism and customer service.

- **Highlights Areas for Improvement**

    Negative reviews can point out areas of your business that need improvement, offering valuable insights you may not have noticed otherwise.

The key to handling negative reviews is in your response. A well-crafted reply can mitigate the damage, address the issue and demonstrate your commitment to excellent customer service. Best of all, you can use AI to do this for you and remove the emotion that may be attached to receiving negative reviews.

Step 1: Stay Calm and Avoid a Knee-Jerk Reaction

When you first read a negative review, your initial reaction might be frustration or defensiveness. However, responding impulsively can worsen the situation. You should stay calm and take time to consider the best approach. Remember, your reply will be visible to everyone and potential customers will judge your professionalism based on how you handle the criticism.

1. **Take a Step Back**

   Resist the urge to respond immediately. Give yourself a moment to cool off before crafting your response. This ensures you approach the situation rationally rather than emotionally. Consider the customer's perspective. While their review may seem unfair, try to empathise with their experience and how they might have perceived the situation.

2. **Assess the Review Objectively**

   Look for valid points in a critical review. Is there any truth to their complaint? Did something in your process or service delivery fall short? Separate facts from emotions. Not all negative reviews are based on objective issues, some might stem from personal preferences or circumstances beyond your control.

Step 2: Respond Promptly and Professionally

Once you've cooled off and evaluated the review, it's time to respond. The way you address the situation publicly says a lot about the integrity of your business. A timely and professional response can not only salvage the relationship with the reviewer but also impress potential customers who are watching.

1. **Acknowledge Their Experience**

    Start by thanking the customer for their feedback, even if it's negative. This shows that you value all input and are committed to improving your business. For example: *"Thank you for sharing your feedback, [customer's name]. We're sorry to hear that your experience didn't meet your expectations."* Acknowledging their feelings shows empathy and respect for their opinion, which can diffuse anger or frustration.

2. **Apologise Without Admitting Fault (When Appropriate)**

    Offering an apology doesn't mean you're admitting to wrongdoing. Sometimes, an apology is necessary simply to acknowledge that the customer's expectations weren't met. For example: *"We apologise for any inconvenience this may have caused. Your satisfaction is important to us, and we always strive to provide the best possible experience to all our customers."*

    In cases where the complaint is unfounded or based on misunderstandings, maintain professionalism and avoid becoming defensive. Always respond graciously.

3. **Provide a Solution (When Possible)**

    If the issue can be resolved, offer a solution or compensation. This shows that you care about making things right and that you're actively trying to fix the problem. For example: *"We'd love the opportunity to resolve this issue for you. Please contact us directly at [email or phone number], and we'll work together to find a solution."* Offering to take the conversation offline is a great way to handle complex or sensitive issues that don't need to be hashed out in a public forum.

4. **Highlight Positive Changes**

    If you've made improvements based on customer feedback, let the reviewer know. This not only shows them that you're listening but also demonstrates to potential customers that your business is proactive. For example: *"Since your feedback, we've implemented [new process or change] to ensure a better experience for our customers in the future. We appreciate you bringing this to our attention."*

Step 3: Handle Extreme or Unfair Reviews

Unfortunately, not all negative reviews are fair or accurate. In some cases, they might be exaggerated, vindictive, or even entirely false. While it can be tempting to ignore these reviews or respond defensively, there are better ways to handle extreme situations.

1. **Respond Calmly and Professionally**

   For unfair or inaccurate reviews, maintain your professionalism. Don't engage in a public argument or accuse the reviewer of lying. Instead, provide factual information that addresses the inaccuracies without sounding defensive. For example: *"We're sorry to hear that you were unhappy with your experience, [customer's name]. However, we don't have any record of this specific issue. Please reach out to us directly so we can better understand your concerns."* This type of response signals to other customers that you're being reasonable and transparent.

2. **Flag Fake or Malicious Reviews**

   If you believe the review is fake, malicious, or violates Google's guidelines (such as containing hate speech or irrelevant content), you can flag it for removal. Google allows business owners to flag inappropriate reviews for assessment. If Google determines the review violates its policies, it will be removed from your profile. However, be cautious with this approach and only flag reviews that genuinely violate guidelines. Flagging every negative review could reflect poorly on your business.

3. **Engage the Reviewer Privately (If Possible)**

   If the review seems particularly angry or unfair, try to move the conversation to a private channel, like email or phone. Once the reviewer has expressed their concerns offline, they may be more open to resolving the issue calmly. By reaching out directly, you can demonstrate that you care and often diffuse negative emotions that might be harder to resolve publicly.

Review Builder Pro can assist you with managing bad reviews by redirecting the reviewer to a private message option before posting on Google or other review platforms. This allows you to resolve the issue before any review goes public.

Step 4: Turn a Bad Review into a Positive Experience

Every negative review is an opportunity to improve. Customers who leave negative feedback often want to feel heard and valued. When handled well, many disgruntled customers will give you a second chance—and some might even update their reviews to reflect a better experience.

1. **Follow Up After the Issue is Resolved**

   Once you've addressed the problem and resolved the issue, follow up with the customer. Ask if they are satisfied with the resolution and if there's anything more you can do. If the customer is pleased with how you handled the situation, gently suggest that they update their review. Most customers whose complaints have been addressed will be willing to amend their initial feedback. For example: *"We're glad we could resolve the issue. If you're satisfied with the outcome, we'd appreciate it if you would consider updating your review to reflect your experience."*

2. **Publicly Thank Customers for Updating Their Reviews**

   If a customer does update their review after you've resolved the issue, be sure to thank them publicly. This further reinforces your commitment to customer satisfaction and shows others that you value feedback. For example: *"Thank you so much for updating your review, [customer's name]. We're happy that we could resolve the issue and look forward to serving you again in the future!"*

Step 5: Learn and Grow from Negative Feedback

Negative reviews can be emotionally tough, but they provide an opportunity for growth. Use these reviews to identify any underlying issues in your business and take steps to address them. Over time, improving on these weaknesses will lead to fewer negative reviews and a stronger customer experience overall.

1. **Identify Patterns**

    If you notice recurring themes in your negative reviews—whether it's long wait times, inconsistent product quality, or poor communication—use this feedback to make improvements. Implement changes based on this feedback and let your customers know that you're making progress.

2. **Celebrate Wins and Improvements**

    Don't just focus on the negative; celebrate the positive changes you make as a result of customer feedback. Recognising improvements will help boost team morale and ensure that your business is constantly evolving.

Conclusion: Negative Reviews are Opportunities in Disguise

Handling negative reviews professionally and proactively is a hallmark of a successful business. While it's impossible to avoid them completely, you can control how you respond and use them as opportunities for growth. Customers who notice that you care about resolving issues and improving your services have far greater trust in your business.

In the next chapter, I'll show you how automation tools can streamline your review requests and reputation management, ensuring that your business continues to grow without taking up too much of your time.

Game Changing Automation Tools and Software

Game Changing Automation Tools and Software

As your business grows, so does the need for streamlined processes, especially managing reviews. Manually requesting reviews from customers, tracking responses and handling feedback can become overwhelming and time-consuming. Fortunately, with the help of automation tools and software, you can easily automate much of this process, saving time while still maintaining high-quality interactions with your customers.

In this chapter, I'll run through how to use these tools to automate your review collection, track customer feedback and manage your online reputation without sacrificing the personal touch.

Why Automate Your Review Process?

Automating review management isn't only about saving time, it's also about ensuring consistency, efficiency and growth. Here's why automation is the best way forward for businesses looking to maximise their reviews:

- **Consistency**

    By automating the process, every customer will be prompted for feedback, ensuring you never miss an opportunity to collect a review.

- **Efficiency**

    Automation removes the manual workload of sending follow-up emails and text messages, tracking review requests and organising feedback.

- **Scalability**

    As your business grows, automation tools are extremely helpful in managing an increasing number of reviews without adding more administrative tasks.

- **Better Customer Experience**

    Automated tools can prompt customers for reviews at the right time, keeping the process smooth and non-intrusive.

Types of Review Automation Tools

Several tools are available that can help you manage and automate the process of collecting, tracking and responding to reviews. Each type serves a different purpose and many tools combine multiple functions. Let's take a closer look:

1. **Customer Relationship Management (CRM) Systems**

    A CRM system helps you manage your interactions with current and potential customers. Many CRMs can automate follow-up emails after a customer interaction, prompting them to leave a review. Popular CRMs like HubSpot, Salesforce and Zoho offer automation features that will send personalised review requests at specific touchpoints.

    How It Works: After a customer completes a purchase or receives a service, the CRM automatically sends a follow-up message thanking them and requesting a review. The message can include a direct link to your Google Business Profile, making it easy for customers to leave feedback.

2. **Review Management Platforms**

    Review management platforms are specialised tools designed to help you track, manage and respond to customer reviews across multiple platforms like Google, Yelp and Facebook. These tools can automate review requests and monitor incoming reviews in real time.

    How It Works: Review management platforms integrate with your website and/or CRM system to automatically send out review requests. They also consolidate reviews from multiple platforms into a single dashboard, so you can monitor all customer feedback in one place.

3. **Email and SMS Automation Tools**

   Email and SMS marketing tools like Mailchimp, Klaviyo and Sendinblue can be used to automate review requests via email or text message.

   How It Works: You can set up automated workflows that trigger after a customer purchase, sending out review requests at specific intervals. These tools can be set up to create personalised messages and include direct links to your review page.

4. **Survey and Feedback Tools**

   Platforms like SurveyMonkey, Google Forms and Typeform can collect more detailed feedback from customers. While these tools are not specifically designed for Google reviews, they can be used to gather initial feedback and then prompt customers to share their thoughts publicly.

   How It Works: After completing a survey or feedback form, you can encourage satisfied customers to leave a review on Google. This two-step process ensures that only happy customers are directed to leave public reviews, while any negative feedback is addressed privately.

How to Set Up Automated Review Requests

Here's how to go about setting up an automated system for review requests using a combination of tools:

1. **Choose the Right Tool for Your Business**

   Start by selecting a tool that best suits your business size and needs. For small businesses, a CRM with automated follow-ups might be sufficient, however a dedicated review management platform could be more effective in automating and streamlining your review strategy. Ensure the tool integrates with your current systems (e.g., website, CRM, or payment gateway) to simplify the process.

2. **Segment Your Audience**

Not every customer interaction requires the same type of follow-up. Segment your customers based on their experience with your business (first-time customers, repeat customers, etc.) and tailor your review requests accordingly. For example, a first-time customer might receive a thank-you email with a gentle request for feedback, while a repeat customer might receive a more personalised message acknowledging their loyalty before asking for a review.

3. **Set Up Timely Review Requests**

You now already know that timing is important when sending out review requests. Set your system to send a follow-up message at the ideal time—usually within 24-48 hours after completion of a transaction or service. This is when the customer's experience is still fresh in their minds, making them more inclined to leave feedback. You can also set up reminders for customers who didn't respond to the initial request. A friendly reminder a few days later can boost your chances of getting a review.

4. **Customise Your Messages**

Personalisation is key. Make sure that your review request feels personal and relevant to the customer's experience. Use their name, mention the specific product or service they purchased and thank them for their business. Here's an example message: *Dear [Customer's Name], thank you for choosing [Business Name]! We hope you enjoyed your experience with us. If you have a moment, we'd love to hear your thoughts on Google. Your feedback helps us continue to improve and serve amazing customers like you. [Insert review link here].*

5. **Monitor and Respond to Reviews**

   Automating the review request process doesn't mean you can ignore the reviews that come in. Make sure to monitor reviews regularly and respond promptly, whether they're positive or negative. Most review management platforms, including Review Builder Pro, will notify you of new reviews in real-time, making it easier to keep up with customer feedback.

Benefits of Automating Review Requests

Automating your review process offers several benefits that will help your business grow:

1. **Increase in Review Volume**

   With a consistent and automated system, you'll see a significant increase in the number of reviews your business receives. This higher volume not only boosts your Google ranking but also provides more social proof to potential customers.

2. **Improved Customer Experience**

   Automating the review request process ensures that every customer receives a follow-up, enhancing their overall experience. A well-timed, polite request for feedback shows customers that you care about their opinion, even after the transaction is complete.

3. **Better Time Management**

   Automation saves you from having to manually request reviews, freeing up time to focus on other aspects of your business. You can rest assured that review requests are going out regularly and consistently without constant manual oversight.

4. **Actionable Insights**

   Review management platforms often include analytical tools that provide insights into your customer feedback. These insights will assist you to spot trends, track satisfaction levels and identify areas for improvement, helping you make data-driven decisions to grow your business.

Best Practices for Using Automation Without Losing the Personal Touch

While automation is a fantastic tool for efficiency, no business can afford to lose the personal touch that makes customers feel valued. Here are a few ways to balance automation with genuine customer interaction:

1. **Customise Messaging**

    Always personalise your automated review requests. Even though the message is automated, it should feel like it was crafted specifically for the customer. Use their name, mention specific details about their transaction and keep the tone friendly and conversational.

2. **Respond Personally to Reviews**

    While the request for reviews may be automated, your responses to reviews should be personal. Take the time to thank customers for their feedback individually and address any specific comments they make. For negative reviews, offer a personalised solution and demonstrate genuine concern for their experience. AI can assist with this by reading the review and providing a response that fits the review content and sentiment. I do suggest, however, that a human reads machine-generated responses before they are sent to your customers.

3. **Avoid Overwhelming Customers**

    Be mindful not to overwhelm customers with too many follow-up messages. One or two well-timed review requests are sufficient. Bombarding customers with multiple requests can feel intrusive and damage your relationship.

Conclusion: Automate for Growth, But Keep It Personal

You need automation tools and software in your toolkit to scale your review management process, but the key to success is maintaining a balance between efficiency and personal connection. By automating parts of the review process—such as sending follow-ups and tracking feedback—you can save time while ensuring your business continues to gather valuable social proof.

In the next chapter, we'll take a look at how visual content, such as photos and videos, can further improve your Google Business Profile and elicit even more reviews from your customers.

The Power of Visuals: Use Photos and Videos to Drive Reviews

The Power of Visuals: Use Photos and Videos to Drive Reviews

When promoting your business online to potential customers, visuals are an incredibly powerful tool to engage your audience, increase your online presence and build trust. Photos and videos do more than just make your Google Business Profile look attractive—they significantly influence a customer's decision to engage with your business and encourage them to leave reviews. After all, a picture is worth a thousand words and, in the context of customer reviews, it can be worth thousands of dollars in new business.

In this chapter, we'll look at reasons why you should upload photos and videos to your Google Business Profile and how these visuals can increase your chances of receiving more reviews and growing your business.

Why Visual Content Matters

Visual content, like photos and videos, creates a strong first impression for potential customers. Google has publicly stated that businesses with visually engaging profiles get significantly more clicks, engagement and, most importantly, conversions. When customers can see what your business looks like, the products you offer and the atmosphere of your establishment, the most likely outcome is that they will choose you over your competitors.

Here's why visuals matter for driving reviews:

- **Builds Trust and Transparency**

    Showing your actual business with photos and videos gives potential customers a realistic idea of what to expect. It makes your business feel more authentic and trustworthy.

- **Encourages Engagement**

    Customers who see compelling visuals will almost always visit your business and leave a review, especially if they had an experience that matched or exceeded what they saw online.

- **Improves SEO and Rankings**

    Google's algorithm favours profiles that have updated and relevant content. Regularly uploading photos and videos signals to Google that your business is active, which can boost your rankings in local search results.

Step 1: Add High-Quality Photos to Your Google Business Profile

Your Google Business Profile has a section where you can upload photos that show your business, products, services, and even customers enjoying your offerings. You should take advantage of this feature by adding high-quality, relevant photos that show off the best aspects of your business.

1. **Types of Photos to Include**

    - **Exterior Photos.** Give potential customers a clear idea of what your storefront looks like. This is especially important for customers visiting your physical location for the first time, as it helps them identify your business quickly.
    - **Interior Photos.** Show off the interior of your business, especially if you own a restaurant, retail shop, or any service-based business where atmosphere matters. Make your space look inviting and professional.
    - **Product Photos.** Highlight the products you sell, particularly your best sellers or unique items. High-quality images of your products definitely influence purchasing decisions.
    - **Service Photos.** If you offer services, include photos that demonstrate what customers can expect, whether that is a stylist working on a client's hair, a mechanic working on a car, or a massage therapist preparing a room for relaxation.

- **Customer Photos.** With their permission, include pictures of your customers enjoying your services or products. This adds authenticity and social proof, showing potential customers that others are satisfied with your offerings.
- **Team Photos.** Introducing your team through photos helps humanise your business and builds a connection with customers.

2. **How to Take High-Quality Photos**

    - **Use Good Lighting.** Natural light is always best. Ensure your photos are well-lit and show your business in the best possible way. Avoid dark, grainy images that could create a negative impression.
    - **Keep It Professional.** While you don't necessarily need a professional photographer, make sure your photos are clear, well-composed and free of distractions. A blurry or poorly framed image can harm your credibility.
    - **Show Authenticity.** Avoid using stock photos. Authentic images of your actual business, products and customers will create a stronger connection with potential customers.

3. **Encourage Customers to Upload Photos**

    Customers can also upload photos when they leave reviews, which adds an extra layer of authenticity and engagement. To encourage this, simply ask happy customers if they would mind snapping a picture and sharing it in their review. You could say something like: *"We'd love to see your photos! If you enjoyed your experience, feel free to share a picture with your review."*

Step 2: Incorporate Videos into Your Profile

Videos are one of the most powerful tools for engaging your audience. They capture attention more effectively than static images, showcase more detail and tell your story in a dynamic way. On your Google Business Profile, you can upload videos that are up to 30 seconds long, which is more than enough time to have an impact.

1. **What Types of Videos to Share**

    - **Business Overview.** Create a short video that introduces your business, its values and what you offer. This could be a tour of your facility, a meet-and-greet with the team, or a quick showcase of your products or services.
    - **Behind-the-Scenes.** Customers love to see the behind-the-scenes process of how your business operates. For example, if you run a restaurant, a video of the kitchen staff in action or how a dish is prepared can be fascinating.
    - **Customer Testimonials.** Video testimonials from satisfied customers are incredibly powerful. Ask loyal customers if they'd be willing to share their experience on camera.
    - **Special Events or Promotions.** If you're hosting an event or running a special promotion, share a video to get people excited and give them a reason to visit your business and leave a review.

2. **How to Create Compelling Videos**

    - **Keep It Short and Engaging.** Since Google limits videos to 30 seconds, make sure to get straight to the point and capture attention right away. Showcase what's most important about your business or product quickly and clearly.
    - **Use Clear Audio.** If your video includes spoken dialogue, ensure the audio is clear and easy to understand. Background noise can distract from your message.
    - **Showcase Personality.** Videos are a chance to show off your brand's personality. Don't be afraid to add a personal touch, whether that's the founder talking directly to the camera or showing off your team's unique vibe.

3. **Promoting User-Generated Videos**

    Just like photos, user-generated videos can be highly engaging. Encourage customers to share short videos of their experience with your products or services. You could incentivise this by running a contest in which the best customer video wins a prize, or simply ask them to add a video to their review.

How Visuals Drive More Reviews

Now that you have an understanding of what visuals to add, we'll have a look at how these photos and videos directly influence the number and quality of reviews your business receives.

1. **Visuals Make Your Profile More Inviting**

   Customers will almost always engage with a profile that has a wide range of appealing visuals. Photos and videos help your business feel approachable and accessible, increasing the likelihood that customers will not only visit but also leave reviews.

2. **Customers Feel More Confident Leaving Reviews**

   When customers see real photos and videos of your business, they feel more confident that their review will be relevant and appreciated. If your visuals reflect a professional and inviting atmosphere, customers will be more inclined to share their positive experiences.

3. **Visual Content Encourages User-Generated Reviews**

   By actively encouraging customers to share their own photos and videos, you're creating an interactive experience that leads to more organic reviews. Customers who upload visuals with their reviews often leave more detailed feedback, which improves your overall online reputation.

4. **Increased Engagement Through Social Proof**

   Customers are influenced by what others are doing. When they see other people leaving reviews with photos and videos, they'll be more inclined to do the same. The more engagement your profile has, the more it grows, leading to more reviews and visibility.

Step 3: Consistently Update Your Visual Content

Consistency is key in maintaining an engaging and attractive Google Business Profile. Your business evolves, and so should your visuals.

Make a habit of regularly uploading new photos and videos to keep your profile fresh and reflective of your current offerings.

1. **Seasonal Updates**

   Update your visuals to reflect changes in your business throughout the year. For example, if you're a retail business, show off your holiday displays. If you're a restaurant, showcase your seasonal menu items.

2. **Highlight New Products or Services**

   When you introduce new products or services, be sure to add updated visuals to your profile. This keeps your content relevant and gives your customers a reason to return to your page.

3. **Incorporate Customer Feedback**

   If a customer leaves a glowing review about a specific product or service, consider uploading visuals related to that experience. This not only highlights your customer's feedback but also reinforces the positive image you're building.

Conclusion: Visuals are a Gateway to More Reviews

The power of photos and videos cannot be overstated as they encourage customer engagement and drive ongoing positive reviews. By adding high-quality, authentic visuals to your Google Business Profile, you create a welcoming and trustworthy environment that encourages customers to leave feedback. In today's online local business marketing environment, customers expect businesses to show, not just tell, what they have to offer. The more visually appealing your profile is, the better your chances are to capture your audience's attention, grow your reviews and boost your business.

In the next chapter, I'll show you how to turn your Google reviews into marketing gold by using customer feedback to add value to your website, social media presence and advertising efforts.

Social Proof: Turn Google Reviews into Marketing Gold

Social Proof: Turn Google Reviews into Marketing Gold

Google reviews are not just a tool to build credibility—they provide invaluable social proof that can be the key to supercharging your marketing efforts. Social proof is a powerful psychological phenomenon where people look to the behaviour and opinions of others to guide their own decisions. Positive reviews are endorsements from real customers, reassuring potential buyers that your business is trustworthy and worth their investment.

In this chapter, we'll take a look at how you can transform your Google reviews into marketing gold. From integrating reviews into your website and social media to using them in advertising campaigns, I'll show you how to maximise the impact of your customer feedback and use it to drive more business your way.

What is Social Proof?

I introduced the concept of social proof in the first chapter. But in case you can't remember, social proof is the idea that people are inclined to trust the actions and opinions of others when making decisions, particularly in unfamiliar situations. Customer reviews are a powerful form of social proof. When potential customers see that others have had positive experiences with your business, they will feel more confident in choosing your products or services.

Here's why social proof is so effective in marketing:

- **Builds Trust**

    People tend to trust the opinions of other customers more than they trust marketing messages from the business itself. Positive reviews build instant credibility.

- **Reduces Risk**

    Buying from a new business or trying a new product involves risk. Seeing that others have had successful experiences reduces that risk and encourages decision-making.

- **Increases Conversions**

    Social proof can tip the scales in favour of purchasing decisions. Whether it's on your website, in an ad, or on social media, positive reviews can push potential customers to take action.

Step 1: Display Reviews on Your Website

Your website is the first point of contact for many potential customers, and integrating Google reviews directly into your site can significantly boost conversions. By showcasing real customer feedback, you offer visitors the reassurance they need to move forward with their purchase or inquiry.

1. **Create a Dedicated Testimonial Page**

    A testimonial page is a simple yet highly effective way to display your best reviews in one place. This page should include a mix of short, impactful reviews and longer, more detailed testimonials.

    Make sure the testimonials are authentic by including the reviewer's first name and, if possible, a picture or their role (e.g., "John D., Small Business Owner").

    Update the page regularly with fresh reviews to keep it current and reflective of your ongoing customer experiences.

2. **Incorporate Reviews into Product Pages**

    If you sell products or services online, displaying relevant customer reviews on your product or service pages can have a huge impact on conversions. For example, if a customer is considering purchasing a specific item, seeing positive reviews for that item increases their likelihood of buying.

You can either display full reviews or pull quotes that highlight key benefits of the product or service.

3. **Use a Review Widget**

   Many website platforms offer review widgets that automatically display the latest Google reviews on your website. These widgets typically update in real time, showing your most recent reviews without any manual effort. Embedding a live widget adds transparency and immediacy, giving potential customers up-to-date feedback. Review Builder Pro has a built-in widget feature that you can embed to display your reviews live on your website.

Step 2: Amplify Reviews on Social Media

The sole purpose of social media is to engage with other people and sharing positive reviews from satisfied customers is a powerful way to do that. Reviews can help you create engaging posts, foster trust with your followers and attract new customers through organic and paid social media efforts.

1. **Create Review Highlight Posts**

   Turn your best reviews into highlight posts that showcase your customers' positive experiences. Use tools like Canva to design visually appealing posts that include a short excerpt from the review, along with the customer's name or profile picture (if they agree). You can caption the post with a thank-you message, like: *"We love hearing from happy customers! Thank you, [customer name], for your kind words. Have you had a great experience with us? Leave a review on Google today!"*

   Highlight posts are excellent for generating engagement and encouraging other customers to leave their own reviews.

2. **Share Customer Stories**

   Go beyond the simple review by sharing customer stories that highlight how your business helped them. For example, if you're a fitness trainer, share a success story about how your program helped a client reach their fitness goals, using the client's review as part of the post.

These stories make your business relatable and offer proof of the impact you have on real people's lives. They're also highly shareable, increasing your reach on social media.

3. **Incorporate Reviews into Paid Ads**

    Social proof in paid advertising can boost the effectiveness of your campaigns. For example, if you run a Facebook or Instagram ad for a specific product, include a customer review as part of the ad creative.

    Pair a product image with a review quote to create a compelling narrative that appeals to potential buyers. When people see that others have had a great experience, they'll be more inclined to trust the ad and take action.

4. **Run "Customer of the Month" Features**

    Create a "Customer of the Month" feature in which you introduce a loyal customer and share their review on social media. This creates a personal connection with your audience, shows appreciation for your customers and encourages others to leave reviews for a chance to be featured.

    Use this opportunity to build a solid relationship with your audience while also showcasing the positive impact of your products or services.

Step 3: Include Reviews in Your Email Marketing

Email marketing is one of the most effective ways to stay connected with both your existing and prospective customers. By incorporating Google reviews into your email campaigns, you can build trust and reinforce your value proposition.

1. **Add Reviews to Your Welcome Emails**

   When new customers sign up for your email list, welcome them with an introductory email that includes some of your best reviews. This helps establish trust right from the beginning and reassures new subscribers that others have had positive experiences with your business. For example, you can include a section like: *"Here's what some of our amazing customers have to say about [Business Name]:"* followed by two or three short reviews.

2. **Feature Reviews in Promotional Emails**

   Whether you're running a sale, launching a new product, or offering a discount, incorporating customer reviews into your promotional emails can make the offer more enticing. People are generally more willing to take advantage of a promotion if they know others have already had a positive experience with the product or service being promoted. For example, you might say: *"Still unsure? Here's what others are saying about [Product Name]:"* and include a few positive reviews.

3. **Use Reviews in Follow-Up Emails**

   After a customer made a purchase, follow up with an email that not only thanks them for their business but also shares a few reviews from other satisfied customers. This reminds them of the value they've received and increases the likelihood that they'll leave their own review.

   You can add a call to action at the end of the email, such as: *"We'd love to hear about your experience! Leave a review on Google and let us know how we did."*

Step 4: Integrate Reviews into Paid Search and Display Ads

Google Ads are a highly effective way to drive traffic to your website and integrating social proof directly into your ad campaigns can improve click-through rates and conversions. Here's how you can use Google reviews in your paid search and display campaigns:

1. **Use Review Extensions in Google Ads**

    Google Ads can add review extensions to your search ads so that snippets of customer reviews are directly displayed in the ad. This is a great way to show social proof alongside your paid search results, making your ad more trustworthy and appealing.

    For example, an ad for a local bakery might include a review extension that says: *"Best cupcakes in town! Fresh, delicious and beautifully decorated – 5 stars."*

2. **Incorporate Reviews into Display Ads**

    When running display ads—image-based ads that appear on websites across Google's display network—consider incorporating customer reviews directly into the ad creative. Pairing a compelling image with a positive customer review can significantly boost the effectiveness of your display ads.

    For example, a display ad for a spa might feature a relaxing image with a quote from a satisfied customer like: *"This spa is a slice of heaven! I always leave feeling refreshed and rejuvenated – 5 stars."*

Step 5: Turning Reviews into Testimonials and Case Studies

Beyond using reviews for quick snippets in your marketing, you can turn particularly detailed and positive reviews into full testimonials or case studies. These in-depth pieces of content can be valuable marketing assets that provide prospective customers with a more comprehensive view of the impact of your business.

1. **Create Video Testimonials**

    Ask loyal customers if they would be willing to turn their written review into a video testimonial. Video adds an emotional element that text alone cannot convey, making it one of the most persuasive forms of social proof.

You can post these video testimonials on your website, social media and even use them in paid ads.

2. **Develop Case Studies**

For B2B businesses or service providers, consider turning a particularly positive review into a full **case study**. Outline the customer's problem, how your business helped them overcome it, and the results they achieved. Case studies are especially powerful for attracting new clients who may be facing similar challenges and are looking for a proven solution.

Conclusion: Social Proof is Your Secret Weapon

Google reviews are more than just feedback—they're a powerful form of social proof that can be transformed into highly effective marketing tools. By showcasing customers' positive reviews on your website, social media, email campaigns and advertisements, you can build trust, attract new customers and boost your business's reputation.

In the next chapter, I'll explain how boosting your local SEO with Google reviews can skyrocket the visibility of your business and attract more customers from local searches.

Boost Local SEO with Google Reviews

Boost Local SEO with Google Reviews

Google reviews play a pivotal role in determining the visibility of your business in local search results. Not only do they influence potential customers' decisions, but they also help improve your local SEO (Search Engine Optimisation), making it easier for people to find your business when they search for services in your area. The more reviews you collect—and the higher their quality—the better your chances are of appearing in Google's Local Pack and in relevant local search results.

In this chapter, I'll go into detail as to how Google reviews directly affect your local SEO rankings and how you can use reviews to boost your online visibility.

What is Local SEO?

Local SEO is the process of optimising your online presence to attract more customers from relevant local searches. When someone types a query like "best coffee shop near me" into Google, local SEO determines which businesses appear in the search results.

Google's Local Pack—the boxed section that appears at the top of many local searches—features only the top three businesses that are most relevant to the user's query. These businesses are selected based on a variety of factors, including their proximity to the user, the accuracy and relevance of their Google Business Profile and the volume and quality of their reviews. The rest of the businesses are hidden until you click "More businesses". In other words, if you're not ranked in the top three positions or paying for sponsored ads, you will not be seen first up.

If you want to make it into the Local Pack or increase your visibility in local search results, Google reviews are a critical ranking factor.

How Google Reviews Influence Local SEO

Google's algorithm considers various factors when determining how to rank businesses in local search results, and customer reviews are one of the most prominent. Here's how reviews directly influence your local SEO performance:

1. **Review Quantity**

   The number of reviews your business receives plays a significant role in how well you rank in local searches. Businesses with more reviews tend to outrank those with fewer, as Google views a large volume of reviews as a sign of a popular, credible business. To boost your local SEO, you should have a steady stream of new reviews over time. Aim to gather consistent feedback from customers rather than relying on sporadic review activity.

2. **Review Quality**

   The quality of your reviews—measured by your average star rating—also plays a key role in local SEO rankings. Businesses with higher average ratings will put themselves in the best position to appear in the Local Pack and at the top of search results. Google favours businesses with ratings of 4 stars or higher, so focus on delivering excellent customer service that encourages positive feedback.

3. **Review Velocity**

   Review velocity is the rate at which your business accumulates reviews over time. Google's algorithm pays attention to how quickly you gather reviews—businesses that receive reviews at a consistent and steady pace tend to perform better in search rankings. A sudden spike in reviews can raise red flags, suggesting artificial manipulation. The goal is to maintain a natural, ongoing flow of reviews.

4. **Review Content**

   The content of the reviews matters as well. Google's algorithm reads the actual text of the reviews to identify keywords that match user searches. Reviews that mention specific products, services, or location-based terms (e.g., "best hair salon in [city]") can improve your visibility in searches for those keywords, due to their relevance.

Encourage your customers to leave detailed reviews that describe their experience, as this not only boosts your local SEO but also provides valuable information for future customers.

5. **Reviewer Engagement**

    Google values businesses that engage with their customers. Responding to reviews—both positive and negative—can boost your rankings because it shows that your business is active, responsive, and values customer feedback. The more engaged you are with your reviews, the more Google will promote your business in local search results.

Step 1: Optimise Your Google Business Profile

Before you can take full advantage of Google reviews to boost your local SEO, you should ensure that your Google Business Profile is fully optimised. This profile is your business's digital identity on Google and serves as the foundation for your local SEO efforts.

Steps for optimising your Google Business Profile were covered in the chapter "Master the Basics".

Step 2: Ask for Reviews Strategically

Collecting reviews is key to improving your local SEO, but you must ask for them strategically. Here are some tips for gathering reviews in a way that maximises their SEO impact:

1. **Encourage Detailed Reviews**

    While star ratings are important, the content of the review matters just as much for local SEO. Encourage customers to write detailed reviews that mention specific services, products, or experiences they had with your business.

    You might prompt them by asking: "We'd love to hear about your experience with [specific product or service]. Your detailed feedback helps others make informed decisions and helps us improve."

2. **Use Location-Specific Keywords**

   If possible, ask customers to mention your business' location in their reviews. For example, if you operate a coffee shop in Cranbourne, a review that says "best coffee shop in Cranbourne" can improve your rankings for local searches that include those keywords.

   Location-based reviews strengthen your relevance in local searches, making it easier for nearby customers to find you.

Step 3: Respond to Reviews to Boost Engagement

Responding to reviews—both positive and negative—helps build trust with your audience and tells Google that your business is engaged with its customers. Businesses that actively respond to reviews are often ranked higher in local search results.

We covered this step comprehensively in two previous chapters titled "Build a Review Culture: How to Get Your First 100 Reviews" and "Incentivise and Encourage Reviews Legally and Ethically".

Step 4: Use Review Keywords to Maximise SEO

One of the most overlooked aspects of Google reviews is the role of **keywords**. Reviews that contain specific keywords related to your business, services, or location can significantly boost your rankings for those search terms.

1. **Encourage Reviews with Relevant Keywords**

   While you can't dictate what customers write in their reviews, you can subtly guide them toward using certain keywords by asking specific questions in your review requests.

   For example, if you run a hair salon, you might ask: "How was your experience with our hairstyling services at [Salon Name] in [City]?"

This encourages customers to mention your service and location, both of which are important for local SEO.

2. **Analyse Review Content for SEO Opportunities**

   Regularly analyse the content of your reviews to see what keywords are frequently mentioned. If customers consistently mention certain products, services, or aspects of their experience, you can use this information to further optimise your website and Google Business Profile.

Step 5: Use Reviews to Increase Click-Through Rates (CTR)

Your click-through rate (CTR) is another key factor in your local SEO performance. When customers search for businesses in your area, they're more inclined to click on results that have higher ratings and more reviews.

1. **High Star Ratings Improve CTR**

   A high average star rating—ideally 4 stars or above—makes your business more appealing in local search results. Customers will almost always click on businesses with strong reviews over those that don't, which increases your CTR and boosts your SEO performance.

2. **Highlight Positive Reviews in Your Business Description**

   Incorporate snippets of your best reviews into your Google Business Profile description or posts. Highlighting positive customer feedback can entice potential customers to click on your profile, further improving your rankings.

Conclusion: The Synergy Between Reviews and Local SEO

Google reviews and local SEO go hand in hand. By gathering high-quality, detailed reviews and optimising your Google Business Profile, you can significantly improve your business visibility in local searches.

Reviews not only build trust with potential customers but also send important signals to Google's algorithm that help you climb the local search rankings.

The next chapter looks at forecasts related to reviews and reputation management for the foreseeable future.

The Future of Google Reviews and Reputation Management

The Future of Google Reviews and Reputation Management

As the digital landscape evolves, so do the ways businesses interact with customers and manage their online reputations. Google reviews have already proven to be a powerful tool for building credibility, attracting new customers and enhancing local SEO. However, the future promises even more opportunities—and challenges—for businesses to adapt to new trends in review management and reputation building.

In this chapter, I'll look at emerging trends and technologies that could shape the future of Google reviews and reputation management. I'll also cover some practical steps you can take to stay ahead of the curve and ensure your business continues to thrive in the fiercely competitive world of online feedback.

Trend 1: Video and Voice Reviews Gaining Popularity

The format of reviews has expanded beyond being text-based as a result of an increasingly multimedia-driven internet. Both video and voice reviews are popular ways for customers to share their experiences in a personal and dynamic way.

1. **Video Reviews**

   Video reviews provide customers with an engaging and authentic way to share their experiences. A video testimonial is often more powerful than its written counterpart because it conveys emotion, tone, and authenticity that are difficult to capture in text alone.

   The staggering popularity of platforms like TikTok and Instagram means that video reviews are much more common on review platforms like Google than a few years ago. Businesses that encourage customers to leave video testimonials will benefit from engaging, relatable content that resonates on a personal level with potential customers.

2. **Voice Reviews**

With increased use of voice search and voice assistants like Google Assistant, Alexa and Siri, the future of reviews may also include audio feedback. Customers could leave quick voice reviews, making the review process even easier and more acces-sible, particularly for those who prefer speaking over typing. Voice reviews allow for natural, conversational feedback that provides businesses with deeper insights into customer satisfaction.

How to Stay Ahead. Encourage your customers to leave video reviews on Review Builder Pro and social media. By offering incentives for video testimonials, you can build a library of rich, authentic content that showcases the experiences of your customers in a dynamic way.

Trend 2: The Integration of Augmented Reality (AR) in Review Experiences

Augmented reality (AR) technology is part of everyday digital interaction for many, and it's only a matter of time before AR reviews become mainstream. In the near future, customers may be able to view reviews in real time while interacting with your physical space or products.

1. **AR-Enhanced Reviews**

Imagine a potential customer walking into your store, holding up their phone or AR glasses, and instantly seeing reviews overlaid on products or different areas of your business. For example, reviews about the service quality at a restaurant might pop up when a customer looks at its entrance or dining area.

This immersive review experience can offer valuable social proof in real time, influencing purchase decisions at the exact moment they're being made.

2. **Virtual Try-Ons with Reviews**

   Businesses, especially those in retail and e-commerce, are increasingly offering virtual try-ons through AR. Customers can sample clothing, accessories, and even home decor in a virtual environment. Integrating reviews directly into these AR experiences means that potential buyers can see what others have said about the item while they are "trying it on", thus helping them make informed choices.

   How to Stay Ahead. Start exploring how AR technology could add to your customer experience. Whether through virtual tours, try-ons, or AR-enhanced reviews, integrating AR technology into your business review strategy will help you stay ahead of competitors when this trend becomes mainstream.

Trend 3: Reputation Management as a Core Business Function

With the increasing importance of online reviews and customer feedback, reputation management is now a critical component of business operations. In the future, reputation management won't just be a task assigned to marketing or customer service teams—it will become a core business function that affects all aspects of a company's operations.

1. **The Rise of Reputation Management Teams**

   Larger businesses will probably create dedicated teams or hire specialists focused solely on managing online reviews and reputation. These teams will work across departments—from marketing to operations—to ensure a cohesive strategy that addresses customer feedback, improves internal processes, and manages public perception.

   Even smaller businesses will start to recognise the importance of assigning clear responsibility for reputation management and give it the attention it deserves.

2. Reputation-Driven Business Decisions

Businesses will increasingly use feedback from reviews to drive important decisions about products, services, and customer service policies. In a competitive market, companies that actively listen to customer feedback and adjust their operations accordingly will gain a significant edge over those that don't. As data analytics and AI tools become more advanced, businesses will obtain additional insights from reviews generating data-driven decisions that will massively increase customer satisfaction and loyalty.

How to Stay Ahead. If you haven't already done so, I would advise that you formalise your reputation management plan. Whether that means designating a person or a team to handle reviews or investing in reputation management software like Review Builder Pro, to ensure that review monitoring and feedback are integrated into your daily operations.

Trend 4: The Role of Blockchain in Authenticating Reviews

One of the growing concerns in online reviews is the issue of fake reviews—both positive and negative. As the demand for trustworthiness increases, blockchain technology is being considered as a potential solution to ensure that reviews are authentic and come from verified customers.

1. Blockchain-Verified Reviews

Blockchain can be used to create a transparent, tamper-proof system that verifies the authenticity of reviews. This technology could ensure that each review is tied to a verified transaction, making it impossible for fake or paid reviews to manipulate ratings.

As blockchain becomes more accessible, we may see review platforms adopting this technology to improve transparency and build trust with consumers. It is something I am looking at very closely.

2. **Increased Trust in the Review Ecosystem**

With blockchain-verified reviews, customers will feel more confident that the feedback they read is genuine, which should lead to more informed purchasing decisions. This, in turn, increases the value of positive reviews and raises the stakes for businesses to provide consistently high-quality experiences.

How to Stay Ahead. Stay informed about advancement in blockchain technology in the review industry. Although its widespread adoption for reviews may still be a few years away, businesses that keep an eye on this trend will be better positioned to adopt these solutions when they become mainstream.

Conclusion: Embrace the Future of Reviews and Reputation Management

The future of Google reviews and reputation management will be shaped by emerging technologies such as AI, AR and blockchain, as well as the inclusion of multimedia feedback and real-time customer engagement. Businesses that proactively adopt these trends will not only improve their online presence but also build trustworthy relationships with their customers.

To stay ahead, businesses should:

- Research AI-powered tools with which to automate and improve review management.
- Encourage video and voice reviews to capture authentic customer experiences.
- Look into AR technologies to improve how customers interact with reviews and products.
- Make reputation management a core business function, rather than an afterthought.
- Stay informed about blockchain technology for review authentication.

By adopting these trends over time, you can ensure that your business remains competitive in the digital age, attracts more customers, and drives long-term growth.

In the next chapter, I'll introduce you to the Review Builder Pro platform, with which you can streamline your review strategies and reputation management. This platform will save you time and leave you to do what you do best, **running your business.**

Bring It All Together With Review Builder Pro

Bring It All Together With Review Builder Pro

After exploring the strategies that can turn customer reviews into a powerful business growth tool, it's time to show you how Review Builder Pro simplifies these strategies into one cohesive process. Managing reviews might seem overwhelming at first, but with Review Builder Pro, the entire system can be set up and ready to go in under 10 minutes. Once the platform is set up, it handles the rest, automating tasks that would otherwise take hours of manual effort and keeping your online reputation management running smoothly. You can respond to reviews and share them on social media in the time it takes to have a cup of coffee. It's that simple!

Automating the Review Process

One of the major advantages of Review Builder Pro is its ability to automate review requests. As we discussed in previous chapters, asking for reviews at the right moment is necessary to ensure a steady stream of feedback. Instead of manually following up with every customer via email or text, Review Builder Pro automates the entire process.

Within minutes of setup, the platform sends out personalised review requests via email or SMS. This guarantees that every customer is prompted for feedback, dramatically increasing the number of reviews you receive, without any additional effort on your part.

It's still important, however, to encourage staff to personally ask customers for reviews at the right time, as asking in person dramatically increases the review take-up rate. Customers, or people in general for that matter, don't want to feel like they are letting others down by declining to leave a review after they were asked so kindly. Using tools like QR codes or NFC Tap and Review technology connected to Review Builder Pro makes leaving reviews easy and quick.

Managing Negative Reviews with Ease

Handling negative reviews can be stressful but fortunately Review Builder Pro simplifies this process. You can respond to reviews quickly and professionally, using AI-powered suggestions to craft thoughtful replies that reflect your brand's voice.

In addition, the platform is designed to help you engage with unhappy customers privately before their feedback becomes public. This gives you a chance to resolve any issues directly and keep your public reputation intact, while still improving customer relationships behind the scenes.

Bringing Social Proof to Your Website and Social Media

As we've discussed, showcasing reviews as social proof is an incredibly powerful way to build trust and convert potential customers. With Review Builder Pro, you can easily feature your best reviews on your website and social media platforms. The tool offers customisable widgets that automatically pull in top reviews to display them in a variety of formats, such as carousels or badges. This turns customer feedback into a visible, trust-building asset for your business.

Sharing reviews on social media is equally easy. In just a few clicks, you can broadcast your glowing reviews on platforms like Instagram, Facebook and X, maximising engagement and encouraging customers to leave their feedback.

Comprehensive Analytics for Data-Driven Decisions

Review Builder Pro doesn't just collect reviews; it provides the insights you need to act on them. The platform's analytics dashboard offers real-time data on how your reviews are affecting your business. You can easily track important metrics like review volume, average ratings, customer sentiment and trends over time. This equips you with the data to make informed decisions to improve customer satisfaction and drive growth.

Simplifying SEO and Review Management

We've highlighted how essential reviews are to improve your local SEO. Review Builder Pro consolidates reviews from various platforms, such as Google and Facebook, into one easy-to-manage dashboard. This saves you from having to log in to multiple accounts and ensures that no review is overlooked. By consistently gathering fresh reviews, you'll also improve your visibility in local search rankings. This brings more organic traffic to your business and boosts customer engagement, all without requiring extra manual effort or cost for advertising and/or website SEO services.

The Time-Saving Benefits of Review Builder Pro

Perhaps the greatest benefit of Review Builder Pro is the time you save. What used to take hours—following up with customers, monitoring feedback, and sharing positive reviews—can now be handled in just a few clicks, even conveniently from your mobile phone. The entire process of review management can be set up in less than 10 minutes, so you can focus your valuable time on running your business while the tool works in the background to manage your reviews.

Conclusion

Conclusion

In this book, I've discussed several strategies you can use to collect, manage, and leverage customer reviews to grow your business. Review Builder Pro ties all these elements together, automating and simplifying every part of the process. Whether the task is to send review requests, manage feedback, or showcase social proof, Review Builder Pro transforms the often-time-consuming process of review management into an efficient, automated system.

I would like to recap the key features and benefits of Review Builder Pro to illustrate what makes it the ultimate tool for your review strategy:

Key Features

- **Automated Review Requests.** Sends timely follow-up emails and text messages to customers, ensuring a consistent flow of reviews without manual effort.

- **Review Monitoring and Response Management.** A centralised dashboard to manage and respond to reviews across multiple platforms like Google, Facebook, and Yelp.

- **Customisable Review Widgets.** Automatically showcases your best reviews on your website and social media, building trust with new customers.

- **AI-Powered Response Suggestions.** Offers intelligent, brand-consistent suggestions for responding to both positive and negative reviews.

- **Comprehensive Analytics.** Tracks key review metrics such as sentiment, review count, and customer feedback trends.

- **Multi-Platform Review Consolidation.** Gathers reviews from multiple platforms into one simple dashboard for easy management.

Key Benefits

- **Time-Saving Automation.** Sets up in under 10 minutes and automates time-consuming tasks like review requests, responses, and reputation monitoring.

- **Improved SEO.** Consistently gathers fresh reviews to boost your local search rankings, bringing more customers to your business.

- **Effective Reputation Management.** Provides tools to handle negative feedback privately, protecting your public image and building trust.

- **Seamless Social Proof Integration.** Effortlessly shares positive reviews on your website and social media, increasing engagement and trust.

- **Accelerated Revenue Growth.** Leverages reviews as social proof to convert potential customers, increasing sales and driving business growth.

If you want assistance in setting up your Google Business Profile, I can help with that too. Once you have a fully optimised profile to boost your visibility that you combine with Review Builder Pro, you'll have a comprehensive system in place to manage and grow your online reputation.

I onboard all trials personally to ensure you're up and running quickly and I'll guide you on how to use the platform and answer any questions you may have along the way.

If you're ready to transform your business and take control of your online reputation, scan the QR code below or visit my website https://reviewbuilderpro.com.au to start your free trial today.

Author's Note: New Software Arriving Early 2025 – Review Builder GO

In early 2025 I will be launching a new software product called **Review Builder GO,** complete with a smartphone app.

Review Builder GO has been designed to integrate into smaller business operations, with a very easy to use and attractive online platform with a smartphone app for running your reviews management on the go.

Review Builder GO will have the following functionality;

- **Reviews outreach**, management and replies

- **Inbuilt chat collaborator** to post and reply to messages and chats across the most popular social media platforms

- **Inbuilt Google Business Profile manager** to set up and manage your Google Business Profile from within the platform

- **Smartphone App** for managing your reviews and Google Business Profile on the go

To find out more about *Review Builder GO*, go to https://reviewbuilderGO.com.au or scan the QR code below.

Please Leave a Review

This wouldn't be a credible book on reviews if I don't practice what I preach!

I need your help so that more local businesses can harness the power of Google Reviews so that they can increase their online presence, build their reputation and attract more customers.

If you bought my book on Amazon, kindly use the Amazon Reviews function in your account or in the Kindle App, and leave an honest appraisal as a verified purchaser. I would really appreciate it, thank you!

If you acquired this book via other means, as a gift or lent to you by a friend, please leave a video testimonial about what you liked and perhaps didn't like about the book. That would be awesome, thank you!

I really appreciate you helping me by leaving your honest views and I will respond to all reviews and testimonials, whether good, not so good, or truly awful.

Please scan the code below or go to https://go.reviewbuilderpro.com.au/book-review

Thank you and happy review building!

Author Bio

Peter Lockwood is a seasoned digital marketer from South East Melbourne, Victoria, Australia. With over 15 years of experience in online marketing, Peter applied his craft both locally and globally in areas such as e-commerce, affiliate marketing, website building, SEO, content marketing, and local business lead generation.

Peter is an international guest speaker and subject matter expert who enjoys sharing his knowledge of building online businesses to a wide audience as well as mentor members of an exclusive global mastermind group of online entrepreneurs. When the COVID-19 pandemic struck and global supplies dried up, Peter shifted his focus to helping local businesses increase their online presence and boost lead generation.

During this time, Peter identified a key marketing gap: many local businesses were missing out on the competitive advantage of optimising their Google reviews and Google Business Profiles. He recognised that reviews are a form of currency, and by neglecting this, businesses were leaving significant revenue on the table.

Peter's management platform *Review Builder Pro* was designed to help businesses increase both the quantity and quality of their Google reviews, while optimising their Google Business Profiles to generate leads, customers and profits. Peter has made it his mission to arm businesses with the knowledge, experience and tools they need to gain a competitive edge in local marketing—all while keeping marketing costs to a minimum.

Turning Reviews Into Revenue: A Step-By-Step Guide to Winning Customers Online

Unlock the power of customer reviews to grow your business and boost your revenue! In *Turning Reviews Into Revenue*, Peter Lockwood shares proven strategies to leverage Google reviews, build trust, and attract new customers. This step-by-step guide covers:

- setting up and optimising your Google Business Profile
- building a review-driven culture to generate authentic feedback
- handling negative reviews professionally and turning them into opportunities
- automating review requests while retaining the personal touch
- using reviews to improve SEO, social media and local marketing

Whether you're a business owner, service provider, or entrepreneur, *Turning Reviews Into Revenue* will help you transform customer feedback into a powerful marketing tool that drives success.

Made in the USA
Monee, IL
23 May 2025